OUR WORLD

THE TAMING OF ISRAEL'S NEGEV

OUR WORLD

THE TAMING OF ISRAEL'S NEGEV

by Cecil Paige Golann

ILLUSTRATED WITH PHOTOGRAPHS

JULIAN MESSNER  NEW YORK

Published simultaneously in the United States and Canada by
Julian Messner, a division of Simon & Schuster, Inc.,
1 West 39 Street, New York, N.Y. 10018. All rights reserved.

Photo Credits

Cecil Paige Golann: p. 16, 32 (bottom), 33, 46-47, 54, 62-63, 67, 68, 88, 92, 102, 104, 109, 115, 116, 118

Israel Government Tourist Office: p. 22, 27, 29, 58-59, 70, 74-75, 96-97, 106

Israel Information Service: p. 20, 24-25, 30-31, 32 (top), 35, 38, 39, 44, 45, 50-51, 55, 60, 61, 64, 65, 66, 72, 77, 78-79, 81, 83, 85, 87, 90, 94, 95, 99, 110, 113, 121

Printed in the United States of America
ISBN 0-671-32353-9 Cloth Trade
ISBN 0-671-32354-7 MCE
Library of Congress Catalog Card No. 72-123557

DESIGN BY LEON KOTKOFSKY

*To the memory of
my beloved father,
Daniel Leonard Golann*

Acknowledgments

I WISH TO THANK Professor J. C. Hurewitz of the Middle East Institute of Columbia University for helpful advice and valuable suggestions.

My thanks are also due to several colleagues for reviewing the material in my book that fell within their respective fields: the geographer William Jaber, Managing Editor, Cadillac Publishing Company, and the following editors on *Collier's Encyclopedia:* Jenkuei Fu, Senior Editor, Physical Sciences; Jana Guerrier, Senior Editor, Life Sciences; and Theodore Zinn, Associate Editor, Geography.

I would also like to express my appreciation to Erna Drucker, Erika Izakson, David Kelly, Agnes McKirdy, and Richard Sperandio for a critical reading of portions of the manuscript and to Erna Drucker, George E. Gruen, Don Hunt, and E. H. Wall for suggestions in connection with the research.

Lastly, I am grateful to a number of people in Israel, both government officials and private citizens, who patiently answered my numerous questions and generously assisted me in gathering information. Here my deepest obligation is to David Ben-Gurion, a founder and the first prime minister of Israel, for the illuminating interview he gave me at Sde Boker on May 31, 1968.

C.P.G.

Contents

A Note to the Reader

Although this book is about the Negev Desert, the Negev itself is a part of Israel. It is helpful to know something about the history of Israel if one wants to understand the Negev.

Modern Israel came into being officially on May 14, 1948, after the United Nations divided Palestine into a Jewish state and an Arab state. The Arabs refused to recognize this Jewish state of Israel. They claimed all of Palestine as theirs, and Israel was a part of Palestine.

Almost as soon as Israel was created, it was invaded by the combined armies of a number of Arab countries. After many months of fighting, the Arabs were defeated. In 1949, armistice agreements were reached between Israel and its Arab neighbors: Egypt, Jordan, Lebanon, and Syria.

Since 1949, the Arab nations have remained in a state of war with Israel and have refused to make peace. In 1956, fighting on a large scale broke out, this time between Israel and Egypt. The conflict is called the Sinai Campaign because it was fought largely in the Sinai Peninsula. The Israeli army had reached the Suez Canal and was on the way to victory when the United Nations brought about an end to the fighting. As a result of the Sinai Campaign, Israel gained the right to use the Red Sea for its ships.

Again in 1967, a war broke out between Israel and the Arabs. It is known as the Six-Day War because Israel defeated the Arabs in six days. A cease-fire between Israel and the Arab countries of Egypt, Jordan, and Syria was arranged by the United Nations in June 1967, but in May 1969 the Egyptian government declared it would no longer abide by the cease-fire. As a result, there is now constant fighting between Israel and her Arab neighbors, and much ill-feeling and bitterness still keep the Israelis and the Arabs apart.

THE TAMING OF ISRAEL'S NEGEV

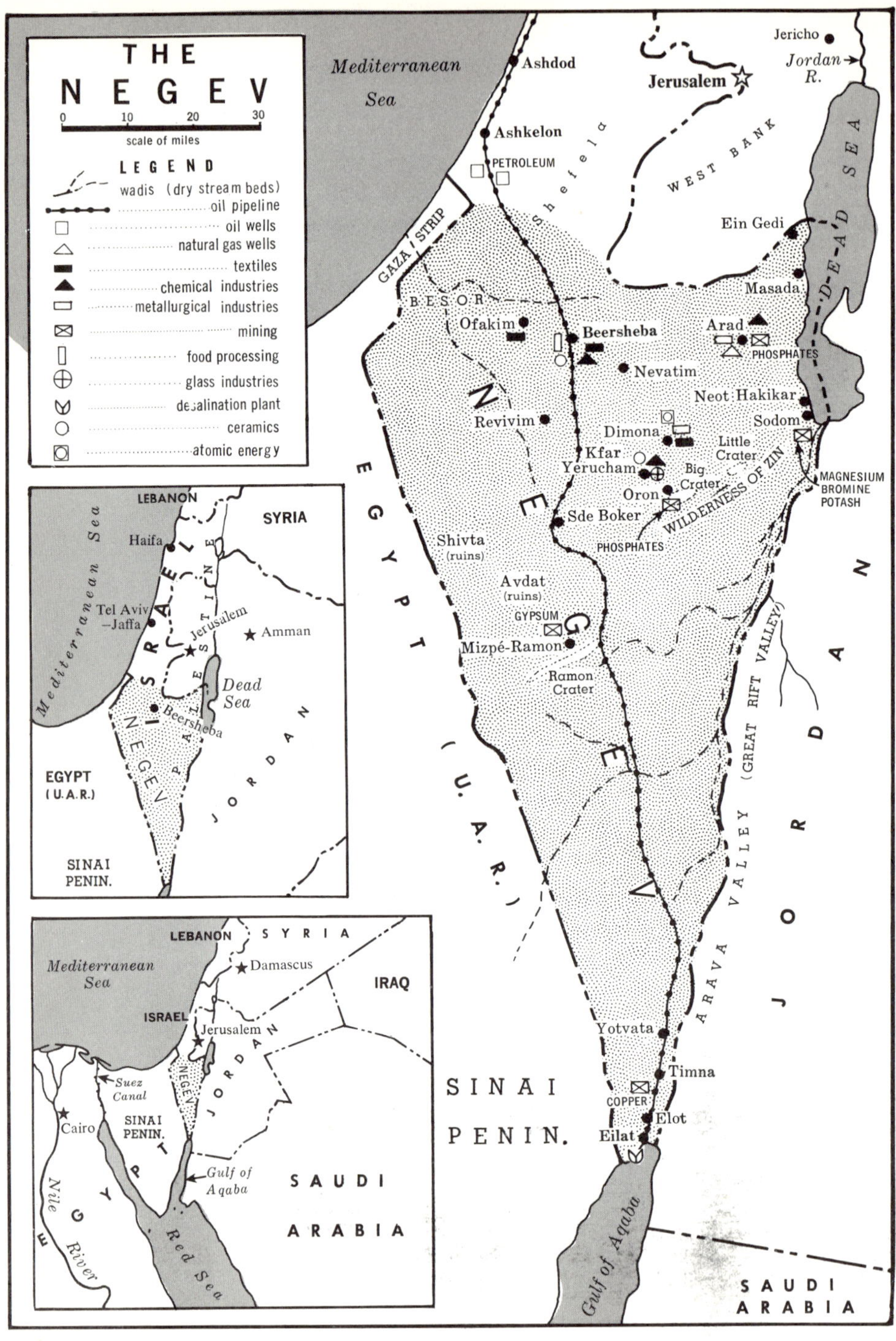

THE NEGEV
0 10 20 30
scale of miles
LEGEND
wadis (dry stream beds)
oil pipeline
oil wells
natural gas wells
textiles
chemical industries
metallurgical industries
mining
food processing
glass industries
desalination plant
ceramics
atomic energy
Mediterranean Sea
Ashdod
Jericho
Jordan R.
Jerusalem
Ashkelon
PETROLEUM
GAZA STRIP
WEST BANK
Shefela
DEAD SEA
Ein Gedi
Masada
BESOR
Ofakim
Beersheba
Arad
PHOSPHATES
Nevatim
Neot Hakikar
N E G E V
Revivim
Sodom
Dimona
Little Crater
Kfar Yerucham
Big Crater
WILDERNESS OF ZIN
MAGNESIUM BROMINE POTASH
Oron
Sde Boker
PHOSPHATES
Shivta (ruins)
Avdat (ruins)
GYPSUM
Mizpé-Ramon
Ramon Crater
EGYPT (U.A.R.)
ARAVA VALLEY (GREAT RIFT VALLEY)
J O R D A N
SINAI PENIN.
Yotvata
Timna
COPPER
Elot
Eilat
Gulf of Aqaba
SAUDI ARABIA
LEBANON
SYRIA
Mediterranean Sea
Haifa
ISRAEL
Tel Aviv—Jaffa
Jerusalem
PALESTINE
Amman
Dead Sea
Beersheba
NEGEV
JORDAN
EGYPT (U.A.R.)
SINAI PENIN.
LEBANON
SYRIA
Damascus
IRAQ
ISRAEL
Mediterranean Sea
Jerusalem
EGYPT
NEGEV
JORDAN
Suez Canal
SINAI PENIN.
Cairo
Gulf of Aqaba
SAUDI ARABIA
Nile River
Red Sea

1:

The Negev:
A Challenge

Imagine a bleak and desolate wasteland that extends as far as the eye can see. Before you lie great stretches of sand and barren plains with only an occasional shrub or tree. In the distance loom bare mountains and parched valleys, deep craters and rugged gorges. Looking at this vast, empty wilderness for the first time, you might think you had some how landed on the moon, so similar are the two in appearance.

Such was the Negev Desert in 1948, when it became a part of the new nation of Israel. Many problems faced the young country. But there was one particular challenge. What could Israel do with this barren, almost uninhabited wasteland?

When the Negev had been under British rule, between

A view of the giant Ramon Crater in the Negev. It is very much like the pictures of the moon's landscape taken by the Apollo astronauts.

1922 and 1948, British experts considered the idea of developing this desert as little more than wishful thinking. They said it couldn't be done.

But the Israelis were not easily discouraged. They took up the challenge of the Negev and began to study the difficulties they had to overcome.

Probably the greatest single obstacle was and still is the lack of water, for the Negev has an annual rainfall of less than ten inches. It is this low rainfall that makes the Negev a true desert or arid region. At Eilat, which is a port in the extreme south of the Negev, a good rainfall for the entire year is just two inches and usually less. The highest yearly rainfall takes place in the northern part and is about eight inches. Compare this with forty-one inches for Washington, D.C., and forty-two inches for New York City!

Israelis love to tell this story about the American tourist who was vacationing in Eilat. One cloudy day the tourist decided to take an afternoon nap. When he woke up several hours later, he learned that he had slept through the entire rainfall for that year.

One may well ask why there is so little rain in the Negev. The main reason is that, normally, winds high up in the atmosphere move in a downward direction as they travel across the Negev. When winds descend, they become warmer and drier and therefore keep whatever moisture they have without forming rain.

It *does* rain occasionally in the Negev during the winter. This happens when the dry winds over the region are pushed aside by cooler, moisture-bearing winds.

Because there is so little rain, the Negev has no streams or rivers that last through the whole year. What moisture there is evaporates very fast on account of the heat. There are only *wadis,* or the beds of streams and rivers that are dry except during the brief rainy season. A network of these wadis covers the entire surface of the Negev.

The rainy season can be a time of dangerous, even terrifying, flooding. The rain often comes down in raging torrents, although these usually last only a short time. When the rain falls so fast and so hard, it cannot all be absorbed by the soil, and flooding results. These destructive floods racing down the wadis are called flash floods. They build up so much force that they can wash away bridges and have even split mountains.

Another problem for people living in the Negev is the terrible heat they must endure for a good part of the year. The scorching sun bakes the land, and sunstroke is an ever-present danger.

In the spring and the fall, a burning, dust-bearing wind out of the nearby Arabian desert often accompanies the fierce Negev heat. This wind is called *hamsin* in Arabic. The *hamsin* is so hard to bear that the Arabs say, "When the *hamsin* blows, one should excuse anything a man may do."

An aerial view of a Negev wadi during the dry season.

Despite its drawbacks as a place to live in, the Negev is of great interest to geologists. Of particular importance are the three large craters in the central Negev that recall the landscape of the moon. Because these craters drop down more than 1,000 feet, they enable the geologist to get a rare glimpse deep into the earth's insides. In this way, much can be learned about the development of the earth.

The entire eastern border of the Negev is located in the Great Rift. This is one of the most striking geological features of the world. A very long, deep depression or trench in the earth's surface, the Great Rift starts in Turkey, extends for more than 4,000 miles, and ends in East Africa. The parts of the Negev that rest in the path of the Great Rift are the Dead Sea and the Arava Valley, which is a depression 103 miles long, south of the Dead Sea.

The Dead Sea is another unusual feature. At roughly 1,300 feet below sea level, it is the lowest place on earth. It is also extremely salty, having about five times as much salt in its waters as the ocean.

The high salt content has the effect of keeping even the worst swimmer afloat. You could not sink even if you wanted to.

The Dead Sea is getting saltier all the time. Every day the Jordan River and other streams pour several million tons of water into it. Although the Dead Sea has no outlet, the water evaporates fast enough to prevent flooding because of the extremely hot and dry climate. When the water evaporates, it leaves behind its salts, which keep increasing the salt content of the water that remains. This great concentration of salt is so high that life is impossible for fish and plants.

Mineral springs at the bottom of the Dead Sea and along its shores also add to the salt content. Salt-covered rocks in fantastic, eerie shapes appear along the desolate shore.

A hazy green in color and flecked with white salt patches, the Dead Sea is fifty miles long and eleven miles across at its widest point. Only its southwestern section is Israeli territory. The rest is a part of Jordan. The heat of the region is the worst in the Negev, with the temperature rising in summer to 120°F.

Surrounded by odd shapes of concentrated salt and salt-coated wood, two swimmers float with ease in the Dead Sea. The water is so salty, neither they nor their tray of refreshments can sink.

If you look at the map on page 14, you will see that the Negev is shaped like an upside-down, stretched-out triangle. It forms the southern half of Israel, which was once part of Palestine.

Negev means "south" in Hebrew, the language of the Bible and one of the official languages of Israel. Originally, Negev meant "dry" and later "desert" or "parched, dried-out land." Finally, it came to mean "south" as well. But whether it is translated as "south" or "desert" or "dry," it fits the region.

At its widest point, just below its capital, Beersheba, the Negev extends about seventy miles. At its narrowest point, along the Gulf of Aqaba, it is about six miles wide. The distance from Beersheba (in the northern Negev) to Eilat (at its southern tip) is approximately 120 miles.

This then is the Negev—the desert that was once considered hopeless for human settlement and economic development. Yet ever since the Negev became a part of Israel in 1948, its growth has caused a surprised world to take notice.

Today, instead of an empty wilderness, there are flourishing farms and productive factories. New towns are constantly springing up and expanding. A thriving commerce has been introduced.

What is more, the Negev in 1948 had only about 14,000

inhabitants, mostly Bedouins, or nomadic Arabs, and a handful of Jewish settlers. Now the Negev supports a population of more than 160,000. And the Israelis say this is only the beginning.

How have the Israelis taken a barren, forsaken wasteland and made it into a region full of hope that is able to support so many people? And what does the future hold for the Negev?

This is how the land of Ein Gedi, a Negev border settlement, looked in 1949 when the first Israeli pioneers arrived.

2:

Today's Melting Pot

Since the Negev was the only part of modern Palestine that had almost no people living there, it attracted the Jews as a possibility for settlement. They would displace nobody. And there was plenty of room for both Jews and the few Bedouin nomads.

In spite of this, the Arab leaders strongly opposed Jewish immigration to Palestine. They pointed out that Moslem Arabs had conquered Palestine in the seventh century A.D. and regarded it as their country. The Arabs did not wish to give up any part of Palestine to the Jews, not even the empty and unsettled Negev.

Many Jews wanted to go back to Palestine because it was their ancient homeland. As early as 1200 B.C., the Jews had

People pray before the Western Wall, also known as the Wailing Wall, in Jerusalem. It is the only part that still stands of the ancient Jewish temple which was destroyed by the Romans about 2,000 years ago.

established themselves in Palestine. Here they lived and worked for well over a thousand years. Then in A.D. 70, their Roman conquerors destroyed Jerusalem, the ancient Jewish capital.

After that there began a dispersion, or scattering, of the Jewish people all over the world, although some Jews always remained in Palestine. During the centuries that followed, a number of Jews in exile kept hoping and praying to return to their land of origin.

Less than a hundred years ago, a movement arose called Zionism. Its spokesmen urged the Jewish people to return to Palestine. The aim of the Zionists was to create a home for the Jews in their former native country.

In 1946, some Jews bought land in the Negev from the Bedouins. However, the Jews feared that the British, who then controlled Palestine, would not let them settle in the Negev. This was partly due to Arab opposition.

Suddenly out of nowhere, one morning in 1946, eleven new Jewish communities appeared in the Negev. They were on the very land that the Jews had purchased earlier. The night before, trucks carrying settlers and the parts of prefabricated buildings arrived in secret. Shielded by night, the Jewish settlers put the buildings together.

During the summer of 1947, a United Nations special committee studied conditions in Palestine. The committee was greatly impressed by what these Jewish settlers had accomplished in the Negev. Despite the overwhelming problems and difficulties, they had grown crops, planted trees, and raised livestock.

As a result, when Palestine was later divided by the United Nations into a Jewish state and an Arab state, this special committee favored giving the Negev to Israel, the Jewish state. Their recommendation was accepted by the United Nations Resolution of November 29, 1947.

Celebrating Israel's Independence Day

After this partition of Palestine, the Arabs invaded Israel in May 1948. The Jewish settlers in the Negev fought bravely, and in time the Israeli army regained the Negev. Finally, with the help of the United Nations, armistice agreements were reached between Israel, Egypt, and Jordan that gave the Negev to Israel. At that time, the Negev

amounted to about 60 percent of the total area of Israel.

From the beginning, if the Negev was to grow, there was a great need for as many people as possible to settle there. As soon as Israel was established, its government began to encourage immigration and, in fact, still does.

Since 1948, Jews have flocked to the Negev from about

eighty different countries. Some made the journey from far-off India in Asia and from Argentina and Mexico in Latin America. Others arrived from Iran, Iraq, and Yemen in the

Jews of different cultures and backgrounds came from all parts of the world to settle the Negev. Their diversity strengthened and enriched the growing nation.

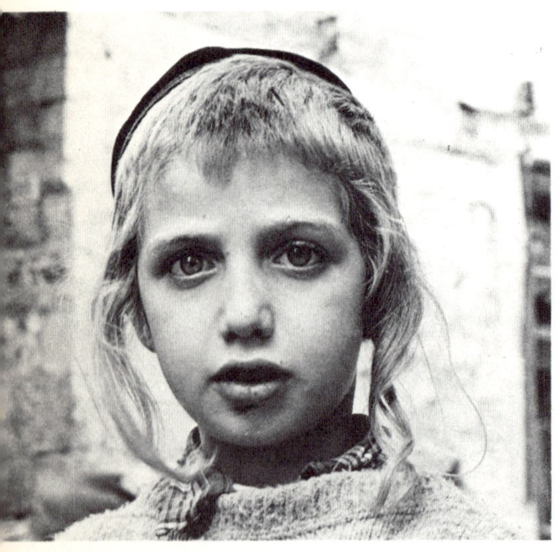

This Israeli child of European origin is blond and fair-skinned. The long curls on either side of his face show that he belongs to the Hasidic sect of Jews.

A sabra (left) and an immigrant from Rumania (right).

Middle East or from Morocco, Algeria, and Egypt in
North Africa. A large number emigrated from Rumania,
Poland, Hungry, and Austria, in eastern and central Eur-

A Jewish child from Yemen.

A Jewish boy from Morocco.

This Jewish boy from India attends a
school in Beersheba.

ope. The Negev also attracted settlers from England and the United States and many, many other countries.

Today the great majority of Jews in the Negev are immigrants. The others are *sabras,* or Israeli-born. *Sabra* means "prickly pear" in Hebrew. It is the fruit of the cactus. Those born in Israel call themselves *sabras* because they feel they are, like the cactus fruit, prickly and tough on the outside, but sweet and tender inside.

In modern times, the first Jews who came to Palestine in large numbers were from Europe. They brought with them certain Western ideas. They believed in democracy and in a fair sharing of their country's wealth. They also felt all men were equal and should be free and economically secure. In addition, they accepted modern science and the great changes it had brought about in thinking and in everyday living.

When the emigrants from North Africa and the Middle East began to arrive, they found themselves in a country founded on such Western ideas. Since they were used to a different way of life, it was hard for them to adjust.

Most Oriental Jews tend to be old-fashioned, while most European Jews are likely to be modern and up-to-date. Oriental Jews weave their lives around religion and the family, while European Jews are usually not as religious or as close to their families. European Jews are also gen-

The sabra, or fruit of the cactus, stands for
the native-born Israeli, who sees a symbol of himself in its outer toughness and inner sweetness.

erally better educated and less fearful of change than Oriental Jews.

There are other differences. While European Jews think nothing of sending their children to kindergarten for three years, Oriental Jews do not believe in sending their children away from home so young. Then, too, European Jews encourage their children to go on to high school, unlike Jews from North Africa, who expect their children to go to work as soon as they finish elementary school.

The coming to Israel of the different groups of Jews is an exciting story. Take Operation Magic Carpet: This was an airlift that brought more than 50,000 Jews from Yemen in southern Arabia in 1949. A number of them have made their homes in the Negev.

The Jews of Yemen had lived there for several thousand years. In this undeveloped country they were isolated from the outside world and other Jews. After the seventh century A.D., they were oppressed by the Arabs.

Deliverance came for the Yemenite Jews in 1949. These people, to whom even automobiles and electricity were unknown, were carried 1,700 miles by chartered American planes to Israel. Their novel journey did not frighten them. They believed that God was fulfilling a promise in the Bible to take them back to Palestine "on eagles' wings" (Exodus 19:4). To the Yemenites, the "eagles' wings" were the modern airplanes.

Operation Ali Baba was another miraculous rescue of Jews—this time from Iraq. A year after the Yemenites were saved, about 120,000 Iraqi Jews were airlifted from Baghdad. Many of them were encouraged to find a place for themselves in the Negev.

Whatever their earlier background, immigrants to the Negev are joining the sabras to form a united, forward-looking nation. Two factors in particular are helping to bind the people together: the schools and the army.

All children in the Negev, as in the rest of Israel, must go to school from the ages of five to fourteen. The state elementary schools are free. Whether sabra or immigrant, the children have the same education and speak the same language, Hebrew. The Israelis have modernized this ancient language of the Bible and made it suitable for everyday use.

As the youngsters associate with one another in the schools, they become integrated. What they share and have in common become more important than their origins, and the barriers break down.

Probably the greatest force for unifying the younger generation is the Israeli army. The youth of the Negev, women as well as men, willingly join the other Israeli young people to serve in the army. The term of service for men between eighteen and twenty-six is thirty months. For unmarried women of the same age group, the term is twenty months.

Young men of the Negev, like all other Israeli young people, must serve in the army.

Since the Six-Day War of June 1967, men serve an additional six months as a temporary measure.

In the army all are treated as equals, without regard to their sex or origins. The army requires every recruit, no matter what language is spoken in his home, to read, write, and speak Hebrew well enough to get along. He must be able to read a simple book, write a satisfactory letter, and carry on an ordinary conversation—in Hebrew.

In addition to military training, the army gives educational courses. Again, the mixture of immigrants with sabras in the army makes them all think of themselves as Israelis.

Jews in the Negev, like Jews everywhere, are also drawn together by Judaism, the religion which they share. Officially, the Sabbath is strictly observed in Israel. From sunset on Friday to sunset on Saturday, government offices, stores, and theaters are closed; and there is almost no public transportation.

Few people in Israel can afford cars, and usually even those who have cars feel it is a sin to drive on the Sabbath. Therefore, they generally only go to places within walking

Women of the Negev also do their part in the Israeli army. Here a corporal helps two women learn to read as part of a campaign to wipe out illiteracy.

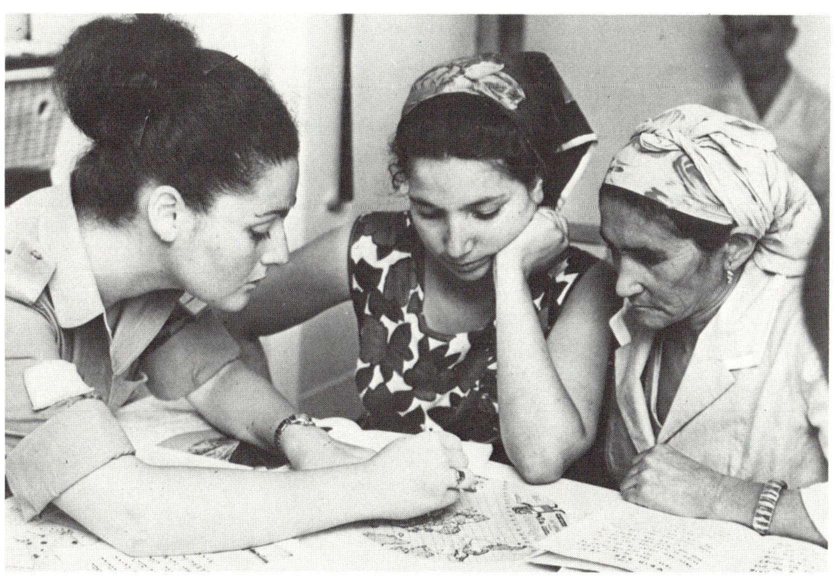

distance. They use the Sabbath day to pray and rest and be with their families.

Because of the heat, the Negev is a place of informal dressing. Men are seldom seen with ties and jackets. Women wear sleeveless cotton dresses, or blouses with shorts, and sandals.

Most of the people one meets are friendly. They are straightforward and sincere. Sometimes, though, they are direct to the point of seeming very frank. But one knows in a moment where one stands with them. They also impress the visitor with their courage and self-confidence.

In the Negev, Jews fill every kind of occupation, from menial to professional. They are government workers, soldiers and officers, farmers, and factory workers. They are skilled and unskilled laborers, waiters in restaurants, road builders, ditch diggers, taxi drivers, teachers, and scientists. They are doctors, lawyers, judges, shopkeepers, and businessmen.

Jews of the Negev differ from one another not only in outlook and manner, but also in appearance. Jews from England tend to be fair-skinned like the English, while Jews from Yemen are swarthy like the Yemenite Arabs. Those from Cochin in southern India are brown like the Indians. Jews from central Europe are often blond with blue eyes. In contrast, Jews from North Africa are likely to have dark hair and long heads, like other non-Jewish peoples of the Mediterranean area.

There seems to be no such thing as a typical Jew either in physical appearance or in behavior. But perhaps there will one day be a typical Israeli.

3:

Dwellers
in the Desert

The Arabs native to the Negev are Bedouins. Their name *Bedouin* means "desert-dwellers" in Arabic. There are roughly 22,000 of them in the Negev.

Bedouins of the Negev follow the Moslem religion founded by the Arab prophet Mohammed. They are divided into tribes, each of which is headed by a *sheikh,* the Arabic word for "elder" or "chief of a tribe." In addition to looking after his tribe, the sheikh is the tribe's spokesman in matters involving the government.

In spite of the difficulties between Israel and the neighboring Arab states, the Jews and the Arabs of the Negev live together peacefully and in friendship. The friendly relations are due to the policy of the Israeli government.

This policy involves helping the Bedouins to raise their standard of living and giving them the same advantages enjoyed by other Israelis.

One of the most important benefits has been modern medical service. This became available to the Negev Bedouins after the state of Israel was established in 1948. The Bedouins used to suffer especially from tuberculosis and various eye diseases. Now proper medical care is bringing these diseases under control.

Inoculation against polio, or infantile paralysis, is also provided. In addition, the Bedouins have free use of the excellent hospital and various clinics in Beersheba. For Bedouins who live too far away, there are mobile clinic units that tour their scattered villages.

In the past, the Negev Bedouins lived in fear of drought. At such times, their animals would sicken and die, and the people were faced with starvation. Now when droughts occur, the Israeli government sends them food and medicines. It also offers compensation for losses suffered during such periods.

The government provides money to buy modern farming equipment and sends experts to give technical advice on agriculture. As a result of such aid, the agricultural production of the Negev Bedouin is at least five times greater than it was in 1948.

Another improvement is the establishment of schools.

Negev Bedouins, as well as Jews, use this modern, up-to-date hospital in Beersheba.

How modern the Bedouins are becoming is shown by their sending their girls to the same schools as the boys. This would have been unthinkable a few years ago. Bedouin fathers are even attending parent-teacher meetings.

At school the children learn to read, write, and do arithmetic. They are taught in Arabic, one of the official languages of Israel. Since the Bedouins are nomadic, a number of the schools travel with the different villages as they move about.

The Negev Bedouins also have the same rights as all

While his mother looks on, a Bedouin child is examined in his family's tent. The Israeli doctor is from a mobile clinic which visits outlying Bedouin villages.

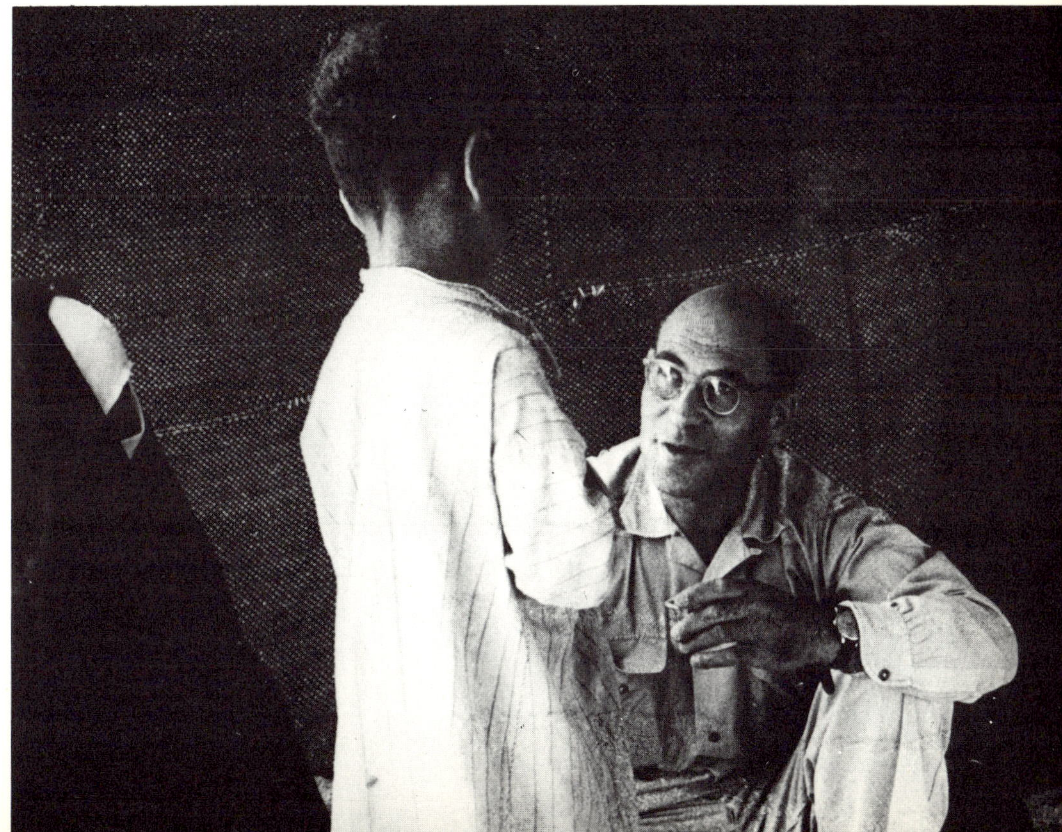

Israeli citizens. They have religious freedom, and they vote and elect representatives to the Knesset, or parliament. They even have their own Bedouin courts to settle certain kinds of disputes that involve only themselves.

If you travel through the Negev, you will come across
Bedouin encampments of long, low, black goat-hair tents.
The Bedouins have lived in such tents since Biblical times.
In the hot summer, the goat hair allows the air to pass

Many Negev Bedouins still pre-
fer to make their homes in tents
like this one. The sheikh who
lives in this tent also owns the
automobile at the left.

through with a cooling effect. In the winter, the rains make the goat hair swell so that no water can leak through.

The tents are woven by the women and can be moved, along with the herds of animals, whenever the campsite is changed for fresh pasture land. This is frequently necessary because the scanty vegetation in the Negev for grazing animals is widely scattered and is quickly used up.

Near Beersheba is a Bedouin village of these black goat-hair tents. One of the tents is the home of Harun and his family. Harun is a good-looking Arab youth of sixteen. His father, Ibrahim, raises camels, horses, sheep, and goats. Harun is proud of his family's livestock, for the chief interest and occupation of any Bedouin is caring for his animals.

The camel is their most important animal. It is used to carry burdens, to transport persons, and to plow. Since the camel has remarkable endurance, can stand the heat of the desert, and go without food and water for a long time, it is very valuable.

Although some Bedouins are beginning to use tractors, Harun's father is old-fashioned. He still uses a camel to pull his plow even though it takes the camel a day to plow as much land as a tractor does in an hour. Moreover, the furrows made by a camel-driven plow only scratch the surface. As a result, the seeds are not placed deep down in the soil and are easily blown away.

Since Harun's village is often on the move, the farming suffers. The villagers' crops cannot be properly cared for, and the size of the crops is reduced when they return for them later.

Harun's family lives on vegetables, milk, cheese, dates, honey, rice, and *pittah*. The cheese is made from sheep, goat, or camel milk, and the honey is made from dates. Pittah, which is found throughout the Middle East, is a round, flat bread. Among the Bedouins, it is freshly baked for each meal.

The Bedouins eat from a common bowl, which is placed in the center for all to use. They gather up their food with pieces of pittah. The men are served first. After they finish, the women may eat.

When Harun and his family have guests, they kill a sheep or a goat to provide meat for such a special occasion. Spiced coffee or mint tea is also served.

Inside the tent, the ground is covered with fine rugs, and cushions for seating are arranged on the floor. Meals are leisurely, for the Bedouins like to linger over their food and have lengthy conversations, which is unlike Americans, who are in the habit of rushing. In the Bedouin view, such hurry not only is undignified but also causes sickness and sorrow.

It is said that nothing anywhere can compare with Bedouin hospitality. These Arabs believe that a guest is the mes-

Many Negev Bedouins still depend on their camels for transportation and plowing.

senger of *Allah,* which is the Arabic word for God. They cannot do enough for their guests.

Like all Arab men, Harun wears on his head the *kaffiyeh,* which is a folded square of white cloth. It is tied in place by an *agal,* a double circlet of black cord. The kaffiyeh provides excellent protection from the sun. In addition, Harun wears a long robe. Around his waist is fastened a belt in which he carries his dagger. Over his robe, he often throws a black, cloaklike garment called an *aba.*

Harun's mother, Aisha, wears the traditional dress of the Bedouin women. It is a black, long-sleeved gown that reaches to the ground. Like other Moslem women, she hides her face in public with a veil. Attached to her veil and head covering are strings of gold and silver coins as ornaments.

Aisha's veil is a symbol of the very restricted lives that she and the other Bedouin women lead. According to the Moslem religion, only men who are close relatives may see their faces.

Another practice of the Moslem religion is setting aside part of the home for the women as a harem. In a tent, the harem is separated by a curtain. The word *harem* means forbidden in Arabic. Only women, children, and close male relatives are admitted to a Bedouin harem.

Where children are concerned, the Bedouins still believe that they should speak only when spoken to. When adults talk, Harun's two younger brothers, Fuad and Ali, listen

Harun's mother Aisha dresses like this veiled Bedouin woman.

Harun and his father often go to the
weekly Bedouin market at Beersheba.

quietly, hoping to learn. They are very respectful to adults
and are well-behaved.

For Harun, Thursday is the most exciting day of the
week. Every Thursday morning there is a Bedouin market
in Beersheba. Bright and early, Harun and his father Ibrahim often go to Beersheba to sell their camels, sheep, or
goats. Harun's father always spends hours bargaining for
the price of his animals. Though it is business, he regards

it as a sport and a pastime as well. He may also buy coffee, sugar, and other things the family needs.

Like most Bedouins, Harun is proud of his people's reputation for piety, hospitality, and skill as horsemen. But this does not seem enough to him now. While his father clings to tradition, Harun wants a more modern life.

One of his cousins, Suleiman, has left their village. Suleiman has settled down in a permanent dwelling in town that has hot water and electricity. Bedouins like Suleiman now work in industry or as full-time farmers.

To Harun, it seems that Suleiman has given up the freedom of movement of Bedouin life. Nevertheless Harun looks forward to the day when he will use a truck to transport what he has to sell to the Thursday market. Unlike his

Today, educated Bedouin youths may read a book while tending their flocks of animals in the desert.

father, he wants to farm with a tractor instead of a camel. He also wishes his father would take more advantage of the economic help that the Israeli government provides.

Having been to school, Harun is able to read a book while tending his flocks in the desert. When he is not reading, he often likes to listen to his precious transistor radio.

Harun may not be the picturesque desert-dweller of the romantic past, but he can now have a life free from disease, hunger, and the constant fear of drought.

4:

Country Life and City Life

When the Jews first moved into the Negev, they established agricultural communities. Today the two major types of agricultural communities are the *kibbutz* (plural: *kibbutzim*) and the *moshav* (plural: *moshavim*). Both can be found in other parts of Israel as well.

Kibbutz is the Hebrew word for group. It is a communal type of settlement where everything belongs to the kibbutz members and is shared equally by all of them. However, the land of a kibbutz is usually owned by the government or by agencies connected with the government.

Membership in a kibbutz is purely voluntary. If you wish to join, you simply apply for admission. And you can resign at any time if you so desire.

The residential area of a Negev kibbutz. The houses are modern and comfortable, and they are in sharp contrast to the bleak desert surroundings.

These kibbutzniks are busy loading the vegetables they
have raised onto a truck for sale in the city markets.

Each adult member contributes his or her labor. This
requires working eight hours every day at whatever task the
work supervisor assigns. A person's task depends on what
the kibbutz produces. Some work in a dairy, in a poultry
yard, or in the fields. Others are employed in the kitchen,
dining room, laundry, and so on.

Wages are not given in return for work. Instead, a kibbutz member receives housing, clothing, food, medical care, laundry, recreational facilities, a paid vacation, and a small sum of spending money.

A kibbutz member is taken care of from birth or from admission until he dies or resigns. As long as he remains a member, he has no financial worries when he becomes sick or old.

Every married couple is given a small cottage or apartment as living quarters. A dwelling unit usually has a bedroom, living room, bathroom, and kitchenette. The furnishings are always of a good quality. Many a kibbutz member also cultivates a garden in front of or behind his home.

Meals are eaten in a community dining hall, although

The community dining hall of a kibbutz at mealtime.

kibbutz members can prepare food in their own kitchenettes. The food served at the kibbutzim is plentiful.

For leisure-time activities, there is usually a library with books, magazines, and newspapers, as well as a social center. Some kibbutzim have swimming pools, an athletic field, or a building for showing movies. Members often buy a radio

or books with their pocket money. A few kibbutzim have reached the point of having a visiting barber and hairdresser at certain times each week.

All kibbutzim have a nurse in residence. The larger ones often have their own doctor too.

The children do not live with their parents. From infancy

The children's quarters at kibbutz Yotvata in the extreme south of the Negev. Here some youngsters aged 4 to 6 are enjoying their own swimming pool as adult staff members supervise their activities.

they are housed and fed separately in their own dormitories, where they are cared for by a trained staff. However, their parents play with them for several hours when each working day is over and usually spend the Sabbath with them.

Free education is provided in kibbutz schools, which are located in the children's quarters. Gifted children are often sent to one of the universities by the kibbutz.

The kibbutz is governed democratically. Its members hold meetings at which they elect officials and decide on matters affecting their lives.

Although kibbutzim are agricultural, a number of them have added both factories and guest houses for tourists to increase their income and provide work for their members.

The other principal type of agricultural settlement in the Negev, is the *moshav,* a cooperative village. Each family, including parents and children, lives together in its own

Babies being fed in a kibbutz dormitory.

Aerial view of a typical moshav. Each family has its own house and plot of land to farm.

Two women farmers of a moshav gather a crop of cucumbers.

house. The moshav farmer has a plot of land, which he works himself. So far this seems like an ordinary village of small farms.

But a moshav is a cooperative because its members both own farming equipment and market crops as a group. In cases of illness, labor is shared. Each farmer's income is based directly on the sale of his produce. Like the kibbutz, the moshav is governed democratically by its members.

At the same time that the Israelis began their agricultural settlements in the Negev, they also started to build up towns and cities. Before 1948, for example, Beersheba was a small Arab town with a population of less than 5,000 Arabs.

By 1968 it had been settled by Jews from about eighty

Children standing in front of the schoolhouse at Nevatim, a Negev moshav settled by Jews from India.

The Ben-Or family live on the top floor of
a modern apartment house similar to these.

countries and had a population of over 80,000 people. To
take care of such expansion, a number of new districts were
set up.

In one of these new districts of Beersheba lives twelve-
year-old Moshe Ben-Or with his family. The Ben-Or home
is on the top floor of a modern three-story apartment house
made of cement blocks. Its walls are thick, as a protection
against the heat.

When Moshe and his family first came from Rumania to

68

Beersheba, they lived in housing that the Israeli government provides free for all immigrants. But Moshe's father, Shimon, worked very hard and saved his money until he was able to buy their beautiful new apartment. In Israel, people usually buy apartments instead of renting them.

The Ben-Or apartment has two bedrooms, a living room, a kitchen, and a terrace that can be enclosed by movable panels. The Ben-Ors use the terrace both for dining and as a play area. The apartment is air-conditioned by a desert cooler, a device which is very common in the Negev and which is also used in some of the hot desert states of the United States, like Nevada.

Shimon Ben-Or is a plumber and, like many skilled laborers in Israel, earns high wages. He is a member of Histadrut, the General Federation of Labor in Israel.

Moshe's mother, Naomi, is a good cook. Usually, she prepares the kind of meals that she was used to in Europe. But Moshe and his younger brother, Hayim, have come to like certain Oriental foods like *felafel*. Their mother has learned to cook this dish and makes it as a special treat.

Naomi also works. Now that her two sons go to school, she earns extra money as a clerk in a drugstore. She really does not have to work, but this additional income helps to buy luxuries, such as the family's television set. Someday the Ben-Ors hope to have a car too, but when Shimon adds up the cost of a car and the high luxury tax on it, he knows that it will be a long time before he can afford one. In the meantime he makes do with a motorcycle.

Shimon and Naomi did not have much education. They want their children to study hard so that they can go on to high school, and perhaps even to the new university in Beersheba that opened in 1965. Moshe dreams of becoming a scientist and doing research that will help not only Israel but the whole world as well. Hayim thinks he wants to join a kibbutz and be a farmer. He longs to see the barren land

Felafel stands like this one are popular in the cities. Felafel is a spicy dish of fried balls of chickpeas, which are mixed with peppers and pickled vegetables and eaten between pieces of pittah bread like a sandwich.

of the Negev turned into fields of flourishing crops.

Because the Ben-Ors are religious, they attend one of the district's temples. In their free time, the family finds many things to do. There are parks, movie theaters, and several swimming pools in Beersheba. From time to time, Moshe and Hayim are taken to see a theatrical group or concert orchestra that comes on tour. For their parents, there are also places where lectures and study courses are given in the evening.

The children particularly enjoy the program at their district youth center, which provides both recreation and educational activities. Moshe and Hayim are also members of Tzofim, the Jewish section of the Israel Scout Federation which is affiliated with the international scouting movement.

At night, when it becomes cooler, the Ben-Or family likes nothing better than going for a walk. In fact, Israel has been called "a nation of strollers after dusk." "Shalom, shalom," the Ben-Ors exclaim whenever they see a friend. This means "Peace, peace" in Hebrew. It is the Israeli way of saying both "hello" and "good-by."

Another Negev city that has had a spectacular growth is Eilat, on the Gulf of Aqaba, which is an arm of the Red Sea. No more than a small police outpost before 1948, it began to expand after the Sinai Campaign won for Israel the right to use the Red Sea for shipping.

The vendor of a newsstand in Eilat reads a book to pass the time. His stand offers newspapers and magazines in Hebrew, English, and French. He has many customers, for Israel is a nation of readers.

By 1966 Eilat's population had risen to more than 14,000. To lure people to settle in the searing heat of this city, the Israeli government has removed not only income taxes but also luxury taxes on the air conditioners and refrigerators so necessary for Eilat's residents. Today, it is a boom town with a thriving commerce, industry, and tourist trade.

Indeed the chief attraction for visitors to the Negev is probably Eilat. Having sun and warm sea waters all year round, it is fast becoming a popular resort. Both foreigners and Israelis flock there. Even in winter, the temperature of the water is usually at least 70°F.

Every kind of water sport is available at Eilat: swimming, water skiing, skin diving, and snorkeling. Tourists may sun themselves on the beaches or go sailing. Glass-bottomed boats take visitors to see the underwater coral grottoes with their countless numbers of brilliantly colored tropical fish.

A number of smaller new towns, such as Dimona and Arad, have also grown up in the Negev. They were established partly to house workers in the industries that have been developed.

Architects and town planners in the Negev have adapted their plans and designs to fit the climate. In some places, the buildings are constructed so that the balconies shade the sidewalks throughout the day. In the extreme south of the Negev, many houses have narrow windows as a protection against the sun and the sand. Landscaping with trees, gardens, and small parks is also attempted wherever possible. Thus, no matter where one goes in the Negev, whether to

the kibbutzim or moshavim or to the towns or cities, one is constantly amazed and impressed by what the Israelis have done with a barren desert.

Aerial view of the small boating harbor at Eilat, Israel's Red Sea port that doubles as a busy harbor for commerce and as a seaside resort.

5:

The Desert
Begins to Bloom

In ancient times, Jewish society was closely bound up with the land and agriculture, and many Jews were farmers. But after they were forced by the Romans to leave Palestine, Jews were often not allowed to farm land where they tried to settle. Some non-Jews thought that Jews could not be good farmers.

The first real chance in several thousand years that Jews have had to return to the soil was offered by modern Israel. Today about three out of every four farmers in Israel is a Jew; the fourth one is an Arab.

The Israeli government encourages Jewish immigrants to become farmers. It also urges young Israelis to study the latest developments in agriculture in the United States and Europe for the benefit of their own country.

To the surprise of many, the Jews have been highly successful in their farming. Using the most up-to-date and scientific methods, Israel today produces at least 85 percent of the food needed by its people. And its agriculture exports greatly help the country's economy.

Israel has done so well in farming that she sends experts to other developing nations in Asia, Africa, and Latin America to offer advice and training. Even so advanced a country as Japan is thinking about introducing the kibbutz system.

A field of wheat in the Negev extends as far as the eye can see. This field was once desert land.

A large share of Israel's success in agriculture has been contributed by the Negev. First in importance is the part played by the Negev kibbutzim and moshavim. One kibbutz that has received much publicity is Sde Boker. David Ben-Gurion, Israel's first prime minister, was one of its founders.

When Sde Boker was established in 1952, it was located in the wilderness, far from human settlements, and was subject to raids by bands of nomads. It also lacked water, roads, and electricity.

But its young founders were united by the will to conquer the Negev, and they rose above the obstacles and hardships. Today, their land is covered by vineyards and orchards of peach, apple, apricot, and plum trees. Poultry and eggs abound. Good results have also been obtained with raising sheep and horses.

Even more remarkable perhaps is the story of the moshav Neot Hakikar, which is located south of the Dead Sea near the Jordanian border. When the youthful settlers first came

Westward ho! This action scene with its riders, herd of horses, and chuck wagon looks as if it is straight out of America's pioneering days. Actually it is a photo of members of the Sde Boker kibbutz riding herd on the horses they breed.

there, they found a salty desert terrain and temperatures over 120°F. in the summer. Outsiders doubted they could exist in such a climate, let alone grow anything.

Instead of wringing their hands over their salty soil, the settlers used their wits. Finding brackish springs on their property, they used this water to rinse enough of the salt out of the earth to grow things in it. They cultivate date palms and grow melons, eggplants, and tomatoes in the winter as out-of-season crops. Out-of-season crops are crops raised in whatever season they normally do not grow. As a sideline, they escort tourists on camping trips in the Negev Desert.

About one person in five in the Negev is a farmer, busy turning the desert into fruitful fields. Negev farmers not only grow food for Israel, but also have enough to sell to other countries. They still have a long way to go, but great progress has been made where once experts predicted nothing but failure.

How can one account for such an achievement on the part of Israel?

As soon as the Israelis were given the Negev, they began to study it. They found that some of the desert was sand and some of it was stone and rock. They also discovered large areas that had very good soil for crops. These areas were desert terrain only because they lacked water. Irrigation, supplying the land with a flow of water, could make them fertile.

Twenty years later at the Negev kibbutz Ein Gedi: A thriving tomato crop has been raised on the once barren land shown on pages 24 and 25. Plastic covers are used to protect the plants from the cold of desert nights.

Aside from the rainfall, which is low, the Negev has almost no sweet or fresh water of its own. There simply is not enough for farming. Other water in the Negev comes from springs or from the sea or is found underground. Unfortunately, such water is almost always too salty to use.

To relieve the water shortage in the Negev, sweet water has been brought from northern Israel. The water is carried across the country from the Sea of Galilee and the small Yarkon River by a system of pumping stations, canals, tunnels, pipelines, and reservoirs.

Known as the National Water Carrier, this system was completed in 1964. The National Water Carrier helps only the northern Negev. The rest of the desert must wait for desalinization. This is the process of removing salt from sea water to make it fresh water. Several methods of desalinization have already been developed, but as yet they are too expensive to be practical.

Once water is brought in, the most widely used method of irrigation is the sprinkler system. More and more, movable sprinklers are being employed. They cost less than permanent pipes and can conveniently be taken wherever water is needed. Since much water is lost by evaporation in the dry, hot Negev, the sprinklers are usually turned on at night when the temperature is considerably lower.

One of the principal soils in the Negev is the fertile loess soil, which is yellow-brown in color and has very fine grains. It is found chiefly in the region around Beersheba.

Loess has one unusual property that can be a handicap. Water makes the grains of its surface soil swell and form a crust that cannot be penetrated by additional water. Therefore, when it rains, the water gathers above this hard crust until enough collects to result in flash floods. Such floods erode the soil and wash away the precious topsoil.

One remedy for this in the hilly regions of the Negev is contour plowing. To prevent the water from running down

Laborers at work on the National Water Carrier.

and washing the soil away, the farmer cuts each furrow around the hill and at right angles to it.

Furthermore, during the rainless summers the loess dries out and valuable topsoil is easily carried away by the winds that sweep the desert. Dust storms choke the plants and expose their roots to the broiling sun.

To cope with dust storms, Negev farmers set shelter belts around their fields, just like farmers in the Great Plains region of the central United States. In the Negev, these shelter belts are usually made up of several rows of eucalyptus and tamarisk trees. The shelter belts break the speed of the wind and slow down erosion.

Planting trees, especially in the barren Negev, is considered an almost sacred duty in Israel. Every year on a holiday called the New Year of the Trees, Israeli schoolchildren plant trees. This ceremony is an occasion for great celebration and is accompanied by parades, band music, speeches, singing, and dancing.

In parts of the northern Negev, where the loess is topped by a thin covering of sand, farming is easier. The porous sand allows the water to seep through rapidly, but the water is not lost. The loess crust stops the moisture from sinking any farther and holds the water for use by the plant roots above it.

The northern Negev, with its good soil and adequate irrigation, now grows a number of useful crops: wheat, corn,

Israeli children get ready to plant trees on their national holiday known as the New Year of the Trees. More than 80 million trees have been planted since Israel was founded in 1948.

barley, cotton, alfalfa, sugar beets, vegetables, and citrus fruits. In the central Negev hills, olive trees are being tested because they require no irrigation. Even the very salty soil of still other parts of the Negev is being used. As we have seen, date palms can flourish in this kind of soil.

Two crops that are especially suited to conditions in the Negev are sisal and a certain type of rush. Sisal can thrive without watering. Its strong white fibers are used to make rope. The valuable drug cortisone can be derived from certain chemicals that are obtained from sisal.

The other crop is a type of rush that is a source of cellulose for the manufacture of paper. It can be irrigated with

salt water. Since there is much underground brackish water in the Negev, this rush is a most suitable plant for the region.

A great effort is also being made to grow crops and flowers for export out of season because they can sell for high

Date palms like these are able to thrive in the salty soil found in parts of the Negev desert.

prices. The Arava Valley, which is warm and mild in winter, is especially suitable for raising out-of-season flowers. These include carnations, gladioli, irises, and many others. Thanks to the airplane, flowers and bulbs can reach Europe

These hardy sisal plants are a boon to Negev farmers because they can grow in the desert without having to be watered.

within hours after they are gathered.

In parts of the Negev it is possible to raise four crops of vegetables a year. The Arava Valley is ideal for growing fruits and vegetables, as well as flowers, out of season.

The Negev wasteland has now begun to bloom and in another thirty years may well become one vast garden.

6:

Industry and Commerce Arrive

At present, Israel is the only country in southwestern Asia that is highly industrialized. A good share of the credit for this accomplishment can go to the Negev. Although dismissed as worthless before Israel was established, the Negev has since turned out to be rich in natural resources.

As soon as Israel was given the Negev, the government appointed prospectors to examine the region and search for mineral resources. To everyone's surprise, they discovered an abundance of raw materials that have greatly contributed to the nation's industry and commerce.

One of the greatest treasures in the Negev is the Dead Sea. It is said to contain between 40 and 50 billion tons of chemicals and is expected to be a source of minerals for the next

Negev industry: One of the potash factories of the Dead Sea Works at Sodom.

2,000 years! These minerals include potash, bromine, and
common salt. Potash is basic in the manufacture of chemical
fertilizers. Bromides can be produced out of bromine for
use in agriculture, industry, and medicine. The company
extracting these materials is the Dead Sea Works, located at
Sodom.

Phosphate, another valuable chemical for artificial fertilizers, is found in a number of places in the Negev. The
most important supply is near Oron, which is south of
Beersheba.

Small amounts of compounds of uranium have been found
in the phosphate deposits. These compounds are precious
because uranium is a rare element of great value in atomic
research.

Potash and phosphates are the principal exports from the

Negev. There is a great demand for both in world markets.

Still another happy find was the discovery of large quantities of natural gas near Arad. This gas is a convenient and ample source of fuel for factories in the area. Plans are well under way in Arad for developing a large chemical industry which will use the natural gas, as well as phosphates and potash.

The list of raw materials of the Negev is by no means exhausted. Glass sand, found in both the Big Crater and the Ramon Crater, is used by glass factories. Kaolin clay is also a product of the Big Crater and supplies pottery and plumbing factories. Considerable iron ore has come to light in the Big Crater and elsewhere. The Ramon Crater is a source of gypsum (for cement), ball clay (for making bricks), and marble of a good quality.

The rich copper mines of King Solomon of the Bible have been rediscovered in the neighborhood of Timna, near Eilat. A major Israeli undertaking is the manufacture of copper cement at Timma. Japan is the leading customer for the Negev's copper.

Also near Eilat are found granite, an important export, and Eilat stone, a beautiful bluish-green stone that is suitable for jewelry.

Other natural resources of the Negev are ochre, manganese, quartz, mica, fluorite, chrome, sulfur, and feldspar.

Beersheba, in the center of a large farming area, has shops

Negev industry: Manufacturing copper cement at Timna.

Negev industry: A textile factory at Dimona.

for the repair of farming equipment. Its factories manufacture industrial diamonds and plumbing equipment, and produce fertilizers, insecticides, bromides, and ceramics from the raw materials nearby.

Among the other manufacturing towns of the Negev are Dimona, which is noted for its textiles and chemical factories, and Kfar Yerucham, where the sole crystal glass works in Israel is located.

The geographical position of the Negev is another advantage where industry and commerce are concerned. Because of its location, the Negev is a land bridge between Africa and Asia. Both continents can be reached by boat through the Red Sea. The Negev also has access to Europe and the West through Ashdod and Haifa, which are Israeli ports on the Mediterranean north of the Negev. Thus the Negev links three continents: Africa, Asia, and Europe.

Because Israel is surrounded on all of its land borders by hostile Arab countries, it depends heavily on the sea and air

Negev commerce: Loading potash on a ship in Israel's Red Sea port of Eilat.

for contact with the outside world. Therefore, great efforts have been made to build up its Red Sea port of Eilat.

Although the total cargo handled by Eilat in 1957 was only 41,000 tons, it had increased to almost half a million tons by 1965. So important is Eilat to the nation's economy

that Egypt's blockade of that port in May 1967 helped to spark the Six-Day War between Israel and the Arab countries of Egypt, Jordan, and Syria.

The harbor of Eilat now hums with activity as cargoes go to or come from Ethiopia, Kenya, Tanzania, South Africa, Iran, Burma, Singapore, Malaysia, Thailand, Australia, the Philippines, and Japan.

A leading commodity in the commerce of the Negev is oil. From the Persian Gulf, oil comes to Eilat, where it is unloaded and sent through pipes to Haifa. Much of the oil is used by Israel. However, other nations can unload large tankers at Eilat, pipe their oil to Haifa, and then reload the oil onto the smaller tankers used in the Mediterranean for European markets.

In December 1969, Israel completed a second oil pipeline, which reaches 163 miles across the Negev from Eilat to Ashkelon on the Mediterranean. This pipeline is also designed to receive the oil brought by giant tankers to Eilat from the Orient and transfer it to the Mediterranean for European markets.

These routes from Eilat to the Mediterranean cost less than passage through the Suez Canal. The Israeli pipelines are also cheaper and quicker than sailing around the Cape of Good Hope. Fortunately, the port of Eilat is able to handle those supertankers that are too large to pass through the Suez Canal.

Negev commerce: Laying part of the oil
pipeline between Eilat and Beersheba.

In addition to the oil pipelines, Israel has been building highways across the Negev that link Eilat with both Haifa and Ashdod. The purpose is to move cargoes across the land from Europe to Africa and Asia and back again.

The Israelis are hopeful about the economic future of the Negev. They continue to explore it for more raw materials. They also have ambitious plans for industrial expansion in the region, and are doing everything possible to stimulate its commerce.

7:

The Bible, History, and Tourism

Since Israel is the birthplace of two major religions, Judaism and Christianity, it is not surprising that visitors flock there to see the many places that are associated with the Bible and the past. The Negev has its share of Biblical and historical attractions for sightseers. Perhaps you will one day take a trip to see them yourself.

Beersheba is a good place to begin. The people who live there will be only too happy to take you to the Well of Abraham, the Biblical prophet who settled in the Negev about 2000 B.C. Of course, no one is really sure that this well is Abraham's. "Could it still be standing in Beersheba after 4,000 years?" you wonder. Scholars who have studied the well say that it definitely belongs to the period when Abraham lived.

If you are looking for other Biblical points of interest, you will probably want to take the tour from Beersheba to modern Sodom on the Dead Sea. Along the Dead Sea you will be shown a particular pillar of salt that is said to be Lot's wife.

Do you remember the account in the Bible that tells how God "rained upon Sodom and upon Gomorrah brimstone and fire" to destroy these wicked cities for their sins?

God had previously advised Lot, a nephew of Abraham, to flee from the area with his wife and children to escape this destruction. He warned Lot and his family not to look behind them. But Lot's wife disobeyed God's command. As

The 4,000-year-old Well of Abraham in Beersheba stands before a 20th-century building.

she looked back at Sodom and Gomorrah, she became a pillar of salt—perhaps the very one that is pointed out to visitors today.

Some scientists believe that this tale in the Bible was actually based on the eruption of a volcano in this region many thousands of years ago. It has also been suggested that there was an earthquake that caused natural gas to escape. Perhaps the gas caught fire and, with the earthquake, destroyed the whole area, including the cities of Sodom and Gomorrah.

Another popular excursion is the trip to Masada. This huge rock plateau near the Dead Sea is 1,300 feet high. It was at Masada, during the period when the Romans controlled Palestine, that a most remarkable event in Jewish history took place.

About 37 B.C., King Herod of the Jews began to fortify Masada and build a luxurious palace on it. He planned to use Masada as a stronghold in case he had trouble with the Romans or the Egyptians.

Then 100 years later, the Jews rebelled against their Roman masters. But the revolt was crushed, and Jerusalem fell to the Romans in A.D. 70. It was then that a group of 1,000 Jewish men, women, and children took refuge at Masada to continue fighting against the Romans. Their leader was Eleazar Ben Yair.

According to Jewish history, these Jews, known as Zealots because of their religious fervor, held out against the

The formation near Sodom that some say is Lot's wife.

Romans for three years. But in A.D. 73, the Romans finally stormed the fortress of Masada.

Imagine their astonishment when the only living beings they found were two women and a few children, who came out of a cave where they had been hiding. They were the sole survivors.

What had happened? The women told the Romans that, when defeat seemed certain, Eleazar Ben Yair urged his people to make a suicide pact. The entire group had taken their lives rather than be slaves of the Romans.

To prove this story was true, Professor Yigael Yadin, an archaeologist at Hebrew University in Jerusalem, directed excavations at Masada from 1962 to 1965. One of Yadin's discoveries was a thick layer of ashes. He thinks these ashes confirm the account that the Zealots destroyed their buildings by fire before their mass suicide.

Even more tantalizing was the uncovering of eleven ostraca, or fragments of pottery, with names written on them. On one ostracon was the name "Ben Yair." Perhaps these ostraca were used to choose by lot the men entrusted with overseeing the suicide pact on Masada.

Near Masada is Arad, which is expected to have a great future as a resort, partly because it is a convenient place to stay while visiting Masada. Arad is high up on a plateau and has a pleasing climate. The hot mineral springs at nearby Hamei Zohar are said to have healing powers. These

View of Masada showing the ruins of Herod's palace and other buildings. It is now possible to climb this rock fortress and see the excavations, thanks to the iron staircases built by Israeli army engineers.

springs too are associated with Biblical times, for King David and King Solomon used them.

Before you leave the Negev, you will want to see the copper mines that were worked by King Solomon. They are about two miles from Timna, near Eilat. The remains of Solomon's furnaces for smelting copper were discovered some years ago both at Timna and at ancient Ezion-Geber nearby by the American archaeologist Nelson Glueck. Guided by Biblical references, he also rediscovered Solomon's copper mines.

Although best known for his wisdom, Solomon was a mighty ruler as well, and his power extended deep into the Negev. His ships transported the copper he mined to Africa, where it was exchanged for gold, ivory, and spices.

Solomon lived 3,000 years ago, in the tenth century B.C. Yet he used a scientific method for smelting copper that was not known in Europe until the nineteenth century. His engineers noticed that the north wind blows almost continuously in the Timna region. They devised a system of air channels that caught these winds and sent the air into the smelting furnaces. The air kept the fires going constantly without the need for bellows worked by hand.

After Solomon's reign, copper was not mined at Timna for 3,000 years, until the Israelis once more began to work the Timna copper mines in 1959.

Also popular with tourists are Avdat and Shivta, two ancient Nabataean towns. The extensive ruins found there

were a guide to the Israeli government in reconstructing both towns.

The Nabataeans were a clever and hardworking Arab people, who had moved into the Negev about the third cen-

tury B.C. Farming and trading were their main occupations.
One of their problems was the shortage of water that has
always plagued the Negev. They showed great ingenuity in
dealing with it.

Israelis today are doing agricultural experiments at Shivta that are based on the farming methods used by the ancient Nabataeans.

To conserve water, the Nabataeans built dams in the wadis to catch the waters of the flash floods. The dams also caught the water that ran down from the hills into the wadis during the winter rains. The Nabataeans then diverted some of this water by channels and terraces into their fields. Some of the water was carried by other channels into underground cisterns, where it was stored to irrigate the farms in the summer.

At Shivta it is still possible to see the old arrangement of dams, channels, and terraces. Today, 2,000 years later, these methods have been revived and used again with some success in the Negev.

The Nabataeans were also traders and had caravan routes to the Mediterranean and to Africa. They established towns along their caravan routes in the Negev. The caravans carried spices, fabrics, and jewels from the Orient.

In A.D. 106 the Nabataeans lost their independence and came directly under Roman domination. Roman rule was followed by that of the Byzantine Empire, which lasted until the Moslem Arabs overran the Negev in A.D. 634.

Under the Arabs, the Negev declined. The Arabs were not interested in maintaining law and order in the region. As a result, the prosperous towns and cultivated fields built up by the Nabataeans were gradually replaced by a wasteland in which only a handful of fierce nomads managed to live. When the Ottoman Turks came in 1517, they did little to help the area.

Turkish rule in the Negev was followed by British control. In 1922, the League of Nations gave Palestine to Great Britain as a "mandate," a commission to govern a territory.

The British saw no future for the Negev, and it remained an undeveloped region until the state of Israel came into being.

8:

Science Makes
a Contribution

Did you ever stop to think that one third of the earth's land surface consists of deserts? These arid regions are the last land reserves that we have. Their development is becoming more urgent now than ever because of the growth in world population. One way to reclaim the deserts is by the desalinization of sea water. This would provide enough water for irrigation and settlement.

To use science in solving its desert problems, the Israeli government established the Negev Institute for Arid Zone Research at Beersheba. Scientists of all countries are welcome to use the research facilities of the Institute. And its findings are available to anyone who wants them.

One of the Institute's chief aims is finding ways and means

to remove the salt from saline or brackish water. But the main difficulty is to find a method that is not too expensive.

At present, scientists at the Negev Institute and elsewhere hope that atomic energy will eventually provide vast amounts of cheap power for desalinization plants. This would make the cost of desalting water low enough to be practical. Then the water needs of the Negev and other deserts will be met. There would be plenty of water, for close to 98 percent of the earth's water resources consist of salty oceans and seas. Desalinization will also free Israel from the fear of droughts, which occur often enough to in-

The control room of a desalinization plant in Eilat.

terfere seriously with the nation's food production.

The Institute is also studying the uses of solar energy. The sun is an enormous source of power that has hardly been tapped. The possibility of harnessing the sun's energy promises much for the future.

Since the Negev is sunny for almost the entire year, it would have a reliable supply of solar energy. More and more, solar heat is being used in the Negev to provide hot water in homes. For this purpose, water tanks are placed on the roofs of buildings. The tanks are equipped with reflectors that focus the sun's rays on the water to heat it.

In the field of biology, Institute researchers are trying to find out what plants and crops can flourish in the Negev so as to grow them on a large scale. To aid them in these studies, they have set up an experimental garden. Here they observe not only plants and crops native to the Negev, but also those of other arid regions of the world. They carefully record how plants react to the brackish water, salty soils, and long, hot, rainless summers of the Negev.

Another scientific project is to find out how much water is needed for each crop and for its soil. Such careful measurement helps to prevent the waste of water. It may also increase the output of crops by having just the right amount of water—not too much and not too little.

Still other Institute researchers are investigating hydroponic farming, a form of farming without soil. The re-

Part of the experimental garden at the Negev
Institute for Arid Zone Research, where scientists
study plants to improve farming in deserts.

At the Negev Institute for Arid Zone Research, scientists experiment with hydroponic farming, a form of farming without soil. Using such materials as concrete, asphalt, aluminum foil, and gravel which require less water than soil, they hope to produce more economical and healtheir crops. The Negev kibbutzim Yotvata and Elot both use hydroponic farming.

searchers have found that the yield of crops grown in this way is substantially greater than the yield of crops raised in soil. Food plants that are especially suited to hydroponic farming are tomatoes and cucumbers. Hydroponic farming is used in Israel chiefly to produce profitable out-of-season crops.

How human beings and animals adjust to the heat of the Negev is also studied at the Institute. What is the influence of heat on milk production in cows and goats? Which breeds of animals and poultry can thrive best in the Negev? Do people who live in hot, arid climates over a long period of time change their bodily functions to adjust to their environment? These are some of the questions that Institute scientists are trying to answer.

Science has also been applied to dairy farming. When dairy farming was first suggested for the Negev, a number of people predicted failure. They said that European dairy cattle, such as the Holstein breed, could not endure the heat of the Negev or produce much milk in that climate. Without doubt the heat did create problems.

In the first place, because of the heat and dryness of the Negev, there is not sufficient pasture to supply grazing cows with enough to eat. If put out to graze, the cows would use up too much energy searching for the sparse vegetation. They would also suffer from the sun. Then too cows won't eat if they get too hot, and this interferes with the milk output.

It was, therefore, found best to keep the cows in open sheds, where they get plenty of air and also are protected from the sun. Feeding takes place at night in the sheds. Because it is cooler at night, there is less strain on the animals when eating and digesting food.

To make up for the shortage of grass in the Negev, grain feed enriched with vitamins and minerals is also used as cattle food. Easily digested, it apparently helps to increase milk production.

Today, the milk production of cows in the Negev is as high as that of cows in the more temperate climate of

Europe. The Israelis hope their experience will help a number of new tropical countries to increase their milk production, which is now quite low.

Animals that survive in a desert without human aid must be able to manage with relatively little water. The camel is a striking example of how an animal became adapted to desert conditions. In the Negev the heat from the fierce sun causes a great loss of body water through perspiration. The camel is able to go many days without liquid because it can lose as much as 40 percent of its body water without any real danger.

Contrast this with man. If a human being loses more than 5 percent of his body water, he is already in great trouble. A loss of 12 percent of his body water will result in death.

Dairy farming: These open pens give the cows plenty of air while the roofs protect them from the sun.

As is true of animals, only plants that can exist on small amounts of water are able to remain alive in the desert without human care. Most of the plants native to the Negev are low shrubs with small, thick leaves and often with thorns. Plants are more likely to grow in and along the wadis because of the water from the occasional floods.

The seeds of some Negev plants can wait in the soil for water for a very long time, even for years. Then when the rains come, they grow and flower with amazing speed. After a rain, an apparently barren area is often suddenly alive with blossoms.

Perhaps the most exciting but little known part of Israeli science in the Negev is atomic or nuclear research. One of the government's nuclear reactors is near Dimona. Its function is to provide ways of using atomic power for peaceful purposes, such as the production of electricity and the desalting of saline water. In time this nuclear reactor is expected to make a giant contribution to the taming of the Negev.

9:

A Look into the Future

So much for the Negev of the past and the present. What about the Negev of the future?

"If the Negev can be developed to its full capacity, Israel could solve one of its greatest problems." This is what David Ben-Gurion, a founder and the first prime minister of Israel, once said.

He was referring to the fact that Israel imports or buys twice as much as it exports or sells. As a result, Israel has to pay out more than it earns, like a family that spends more than its income.

Despite this, there is room for hope. The nations of Asia and Africa, except for Japan, do not yet have much industry. The Negev, therefore, has a chance to become a great

David Ben-Gurion, grand old man of
Israel and its first Prime Minister.

industrial center, supplying the needs of the peoples of Asia and Africa. If the Israelis can accomplish this, they will have enough income to support themselves. In other words, they will have economic independence.

Another Israeli ambition is the full agricultural development of the Negev. This would make it possible for Israel to produce enough additional food to feed its entire population.

There is one huge obstacle to these grand plans for the Negev—the acute shortage of fresh water in the region. If the population is to increase and if agriculture and industry are to grow, much more water is needed.

Yet Israelis think this problem can be overcome. "American engineers have told me," Ben-Gurion said in 1968, "that within only a few years atomic power will be cheaper than electric power. This means that the inexpensive desalinization of sea water by atomic power can be the solution."

The Israelis see the Negev in relation not only to themselves, but to the world as well. They say that if their plans in the Negev succeed, this should help to solve great problems in Africa and Asia. Large areas of India and Egypt, for instance, are deserts. Perhaps the example of the Jews in the Negev will help these people to cultivate their deserts too.

Israelis also like to compare their Negev to the American West as it was one hundred and fifty years ago. The Negev is the Israeli frontier, as the West was ours. They hope to reclaim it, as we Americans developed our West, by pioneering and science. A vistor leaves Israel feeling sure that its people too will succeed.

Index